A CONSUMER'S GUIDE TO
ESTATE PLANNING

James P. Shields, Esquire
Thomas J. Boris, Esquire
The Elder Law Offices of Shields & Boris
109 VIP Drive
Suite 102
Wexford, PA 15090
724-934-5044
724-934-3080 Fax
1-800-879-0984 Toll Free

Printed in the United States of America.
Second Edition

ISBN: 978-1-59571-309-4

Word Association Publishers
205 5th Avenue
Tarentum, PA 15084
www.wordassociation.com

FOREWORD

I have to confess, when I first started doing estate planning work 16 years ago, I never recommended a Revocable Living Trust. Why not, you ask? Out of ignorance. My boss at the time had been preparing Wills for 25 years and going through probate for 25 years. He, like many attorneys, was comfortable with Wills, was comfortable with probate and was making money from it. He did not want to invest the time to learn something new. Many attorneys are just set in their ways and will never change.

I was told that Trusts were not necessary, were an added expense, were a "gimmick" and really did not save money. That was until a long-trusted older friend told me he got a Revocable Living Trust. He told me a Trust avoided probate, was inexpensive, easy to change, avoided attorney's fees for probating an estate and reduced the time for administrating an estate. I was skeptical of his claims but since he was a long trusted older friend, I figured I needed to investigate this Revocable Living Trust to find the truth and make sure my friend was not getting ripped off.

So what was the truth about these Revocable Living Trusts? When I began to research, I read everything I could on Revocable Living Trusts, but probate attorneys wrote most legal books. The books said that my client's claims were right and that Trusts could do what my client said. In spite of that, the probate attorneys said that the Revocable Living Trust was not necessary.

The Trust could save money, save time and avoid probate. That sounded good to me. I knew I charged between 3-7% of the gross estate. Saving the client's family this kind of money would greatly benefit them. It took me a while to figure it out but I finally did. The probate attorneys did not want to recommend Living Trusts because they wanted to probate estates and earn the attorney's fee from probating the estate. The probate attorneys had a vested interest in probating the estate. No matter how beneficial a Revocable Trust appeared to be, the probate attorneys just would not give their seal of approval.

Since so many attorneys and financial advisors simply dismiss Trusts because they do not understand their value as an estate planning tool in the appropriate situation, we wrote this guide to offer the information directly to the consumer. As an informed consumer, you can better make a decision as to what estate planning tool, such as a Trust, may best serve your estate planning needs.

INTRODUCTION

We wrote this book for two reasons. Number one: we were tired of the differing opinions, misunderstandings, and confusion in the marketplace and quite frankly, outright lies that some advisors are telling their clients. By advisors, I mean both financial and attorneys. For example, one nationally known non-attorney financial advisor says that everyone should have a Revocable Living Trust to avoid probate, reduce attorney fees and reduce taxes. Another respected non-attorney local financial advisor says that probate is "no big deal" and that no one should use a Revocable Living Trust. These are two diametrically opposed opinions. So who is right?

It is our opinion that since it depends on the facts of the situation, you should avail yourself of all of your options prior to making a decision. In Pennsylvania, for example, if all your assets have beneficiaries or if your entire estate is less than $100,000, then for reasons we will discuss more fully later in this book, you do not need a Revocable Living Trust. Conversely, there are situations that beg for one to consider the use of a Revocable Living Trust to accomplish their estate planning goals. For example, if you have real estate, such as a home, timeshares, a second home, or condominiums in more than one state, you would have a probate court proceeding and typically an attorney in each of the states involved. This can be expensive and inconvenient for the person in charge of settling the estate. Two probates, two sets of attorneys and two sets of attorney fees are not better than one. Therefore, any advisor who states that you always need a Trust or any adviser who states that you never need a Trust is lying to their clients and potentially doing their clients and their families a great disservice by not properly educating them about the advantages in their situation of using a Revocable Living Trust.

Interestingly, and maybe for their own self-interest, the non-attorney financial planner offers Revocable Living Trust packages for sale on her website. Ironically, the non-attorney financial advisor who says no one needs a Trust and that probate is "no big deal" recommends that clients place beneficiaries on all their accounts, even non-qualified accounts, to avoid probate. I use this as an example as to why there is so much confusion in the marketplace. What we want to do is give you the facts and let you make up your own mind.

The second reason we have written this book is to correct the lack of what we consider consumer friendly books or advice in the marketplace about elder law and estate planning. Most attorneys feel they have to prove how smart they are by writing or speaking in legalese. The attorney may feel superior by using this language but all it creates is confusion for the client. So many times we hear from clients that they had read something or had met with an attorney and were more confused after meeting the attorney than before.

Many clients and financial planners attend our seminars or meet with us and afterwards state how much they enjoyed our ability to simplify things and make elder law and estate planning so clear that anyone can understand it. This allows our clients to make an informed decision about their own estate plan.

We want this book to be a tool that financial planners and consumers can use as a down to earth primer on estate planning and elder law.

What this book is not is a definitive academic legal treatise for attorneys on estate planning and elder law. We will not delve into detailed case law, technically complicated legalese that sounds good (and is expensive) but only makes sense for a client with an estate over $5,000,000. We will not attempt to make you a legal expert.

What we want to accomplish is to educate you about the facts and the estate planning options that are available to you based on your situation. This will allow you to make informed decisions about your own estate plan and what type of attorney you should consider working with. **But remember: although my firm has prepared thousands of estate plans, no two have ever been alike.** Every family is different; therefore, every estate plan we create is different.

The other thing we want to do is alert you to some potential issues or legal pitfalls that you can fall into. Many attorneys or financial planners do not even know many pitfalls exist. We will also give you some tools such as checklists you can use to gather the information necessary to begin your own estate plan.

We will try to simplify complicated legal concepts through the use of stories and examples. We will also identify some pitfalls by illustrating some messes we have had to clean up for clients in the past.

One of the questions I frequently get is, "Why do you practice in this area of law; why aren't you like one of those attorneys on Boston Legal who are in the courtroom every day?" Well, back when I was in my third year of law school at Notre Dame, my mom suddenly passed away. Since I was in law school, the entire family came to me to see what had to be done from a legal standpoint after she passed away. They teach you a lot of things in law school. They teach you how to read and how to write but not the practical things like what to do to get control of mom's checking account after she dies.

I had to rely on other attorneys to walk me step-by-step through the process of what had to be done to settle my mother's estate. What further complicated the situation was that my mom had no legal documents in place and I had no idea what assets, if any, she had in place. After experiencing the troubles I had with my mother's estate, I wanted to help other people avoid the same problems and to be there to walk their family members step-by-step through what has to happen when a loved one becomes incapacitated, needs skilled care or passes away.

Let's face it: thankfully, most people only have to experience the above problems once or twice in a lifetime while settling an estate for a parent, relative or a spouse. Our office deals with these issues every day. What we want to accomplish is to allow our clients to educate themselves about what would be the best way to set up their estate plan, implement the proper plan, be there to help the surviving spouse and, God willing, be there to help the family settle the estate properly upon their passing.

With this book, we hope to expand our voice to even more consumers to educate them about how they should set up their estate plan.

By way of my background, I grew up in Pittsburgh, Pennsylvania, and graduated cum laude from St. Francis College of Loretto, Pennsylvania, in 1990. I went to Law School at Notre Dame, graduated in 1993 and have practiced in this area ever since. Our law firm's purpose is to protect our client's legacy. Whether the goal is to protect a legacy from unnecessary taxes or unnecessary legal fees, nursing home expenses or obtain hard earned veterans benefits for non-service related disabilities, we can help families reach these goals.

We don't practice criminal law or family law. Elder law is all we do. I am the proud father of five children, Madeline, Catherine, Elizabeth, Jackson and Jameson. I am married to the greatest person in the world, Denise. My family keeps me grounded and reminds me that family is the most important part of my life.

My law partner and co-author, Thomas J. Boris, Esquire is an accomplished attorney and great friend who took a slightly different path. He, too, grew up in Western Pennsylvania. He went to Washington & Jefferson for an undergraduate degree and clerked for a local law firm while at school. At graduation, he wasn't sure about law school, so he obtained his paralegal certificate from Duquesne University and went to work as a paralegal.

Tom soon realized that a paralegal does all the work and the attorney makes all the money, so he entered law school at Duquesne University and obtained his degree. Tom also practices exclusively in the area of Elder Law. He is married to his attorney wife, Stephanie, and has two sons, Thomas Lee and Nicholas Tyler.

CHAPTER 1
ESTATE PLANNING 101

Before we can talk about estate planning, we first have to define what is "estate planning".

Estate planning is deciding what happens to you and your possessions if you become incapacitated, if you are on your deathbed or if you pass away. My grandmother always said, "Clean up your own mess." Sometimes the simplest advice is the best. Essentially, estate planning is cleaning up your own mess.

One of the problems with my Mom's estate in 1992 was the fact that she had nothing in place. She had nothing in writing, no Will, and no list of bank accounts, life insurance or assets. Because she did not clean up her own mess, I had to first find everything and then clean up her mess for her. She should have taken her own mother's advice and cleaned up her own mess.

Now I know what some of you are thinking. It would be a lot of work for you to gather together and list all your assets, investments and life insurance. Speaking from experience, **if it's hard for you to account for your possessions and it's your "stuff," imagine how hard it would be for someone else to come in, having no idea of the location of your "stuff" and having to clean up your mess.**

With my mom's estate, I spent over four months going through every piece of correspondence, mail, and paperwork

11

from her "old steel box" in order to try to find any asset to pay for the funeral. As my Mom had died suddenly, I not only had to care for my younger sister and brother, but also had to deal with my own emotional pain while finishing my last year of law school. On top of that, I had to find bills (they were easy to find), and find money to pay them (much more difficult). The worst part was that every time I went through her "stuff" I relived the emotional pain of her death. I feel, and many of my clients have felt that they did not finish mourning until they were done administering the estate.

In addition, since nothing was in place, I had to make several difficult decisions. The first was deciding on a casket. Before I realized we had no money to pay for a funeral, the undertaker said something that I understood to be, "So do you want the cheapest casket for your Mom?" What could I say? Of course, I did not get the cheapest casket. (As an aside, but for the gifts from friends, family and Notre Dame, we could not have paid for the funeral. Thanks to them and an understanding funeral director, we were able to pay the bills eventually).

Buying "in need" is a very difficult position to be in to negotiate. If you buy and take care of things "pre-need," you can negotiate, you can make sure your wishes are carried out and you make it easier on your family. The more planning you do ahead of time, the less mess you leave for someone else to clean up.

To help you organize your affairs, as Exhibit 1, we have

attached what we call an Estate Organizer. This form will help you organize your assets and affairs so that if you pass away, or worse yet, if you become incapacitated, your family knows where to find your assets. The Estate Organizer gives you a place to list everything from where you keep your tax records, where you bank, your advisors and even the name of any funeral or burial requests that you may have.

The first step in estate planning is to identify your assets. So after we have identified you, your family and your stuff, what are common estate planning goals? We have found the most common estate planning goals are to:

- Retain control of your property;
- Protect you, your family and your assets if you need nursing home care;
- Obtain for you all the benefits to which you are rightly entitled; and
- When you die, to get your assets to the people you love without any unnecessary cost, taxes or delay.

Why do we make an estate plan? Maybe you have an 18-year-old grandchild who you have high hopes for and want to take care of but because of his dyed-red spiky hair, he is going through his phase, you are not thrilled about handing your assets to this person with no strings attached. Maybe a child is going through a divorce or having debt problems. **Why have your lifetime of hard work go to waste or be spent in no time?**

By the way, the generation before my generation was a

generation of savers. Because of the lessons of the Depression, their parents taught them how to save. My generation, Generation X is what I call the "Microwave Generation." "We want everything now!" So while credit is easy, we buy everything now and will figure out how to pay for it later. **We will spend your money faster than you ever dreamed!** An estate plan is simply planning to address these concerns. But before we can address what an estate plan is, we must answer the question, "What is an estate?"

Why do we hear so much about estate planning now? The main reason is that the Depression Era generation had their prime earning years wiped out by the Depression and World War II. The house they bought for $5,000 in 1935 was worth $20,000 when they passed away in 1975. They did not have the benefit of IRA's and mutual funds. Many times they have a "nickel" life insurance policy and little else. In general, the estates were relatively small and not that expensive to settle.

However, the one thing the Depression era generation taught the next generation was how to save money. The next generation bought a home for $40,000, which is now worth $200,000. They have investments in mutual funds. They have large IRA's, annuities, and life insurance policies. Since this generation generally has significantly more money, the estate plans are more sophisticated and expensive. Since more and more people have sufficient assets to need an estate plan, you hear more about estate planning every day.

CHAPTER 2
WHAT IS AN ESTATE?

Your estate is simply all of your assets. Your personal property, real estate, cash, stocks, bonds, IRA's, annuities and life insurance. Now every day I hear clients say, "I am not a Rockefeller or a Carnegie, so why do I need an estate plan?" I then ask them about their assets and the conversation goes something like this:

"Do you have a home?"

"Yes."

"What is the value?"

"$200,000."

"Do you have any bank accounts?"

"Yes, we have a checking, a savings and a few CD's."

"How much do you have in the bank?"

"About $100,000 counting the CD's."

"Do you have any stock or brokerage amounts or mutual funds that are part of an IRA?"

"Yes we have about $80,000 in stocks, bonds and mutual funds in a brokerage account."

"Do you have any IRA's or annuities?"

"Yes, my wife and I each have $100,000 in IRA's and another $75,000 in an annuity."

"Do you have any life insurance?"

"Well, I have an old $50,000 plus another $25,000 through my old employer and my wife has a $50,000 policy

15

and an old policy from her parents for $5,000."

Before the client knows it, we have a $200,000, $300,000, $500,000 or $1,000,000 estate. I have never had a client estimate the size of their estate and then add up the actual number later to find the real number to be smaller than the estimate. The lesson is that you may have a larger estate than you think. If you haven't added up your "stuff" in a while, it is a great exercise to go through. If you go through and add everything up, you might be pleasantly surprised. To help you go through this exercise, we have attached an asset inventory form as Exhibit B that can help you add up your assets. I know you are thinking, "Boy, it's work to find and add up all my stuff." **Again, I remind you that if it's your stuff and you can't find it, how is anyone else going to find it?**

CHAPTER 3
WHAT IS AN ESTATE PLAN?

An estate plan is simply a plan for what happens to you and your possessions if you become incapacitated or pass away and more importantly, who makes that decision.

An estate plan is how you decide how your estate will pass to your heirs. Will "probate" i.e., the court system, be involved? The plan will determine the tax consequences of your estate. It will determine who will make decisions if you cannot make them for yourself. It will determine whether your estate will be protected from long-term care expenses and who your beneficiaries will be.

There are several types of plans and we will discuss the most popular. Among these plans:

No Plan;

A Will;

Joint Ownership;

Beneficiary Designation;

Gifting;

Living Trusts;

Asset Protection Plans;

Emergency Plans.

But before we talk about what happens when you die, we must first talk about what happens if you live! Isn't that more important? Becoming incapacitated is a fate that many people consider to be worse than death. Without proper planning, this can create a legal and financial nightmare.

If you have an asset, such as an IRA and you become incapacitated, no one can manage or withdraw money from that IRA unless you have a Financial Power of Attorney in place. This means that even if you need money to pay bills or if the market is collapsing and your accounts need to be reallocated, no one can reallocate or access your account.

Now I realize that some of you are thinking, "I am married, so my spouse can manage my affairs." That may be true for certain joint accounts such as bank accounts, but it's not true for any individual account such as individual IRA's, 401(k) accounts, 403(b) accounts, Roth IRA's, individual bank accounts, individual annuities, individual stocks or individual investments.

Please note that even though either owner of the account can cash in a joint brokerage account, the check from the liquidation would be issued in joint name. This means both owners of the account would have to endorse the check. However, if one spouse is incapacitated how can they endorse the check?

The problem can even be worse. While it is difficult enough that neither your family nor your spouse will be able to touch your individual accounts, they also will not be able to sell any real property you own.

Let me illustrate by an example. Let's say dad is incapacitated and in a nursing home and mom is living in the big house by herself. Mom decides the house is too big and wants to sell it. If mom finds a buyer for the property, the problem is that dad can't sign the deed. Without a Power of Attorney, mom cannot just sign dad's name. So what is mom to do?

In most states, mom would have to petition the court to become guardian of dad and dad's estate. In this procedure the court gives mom the authority to sign dad's name. The problem with this process is that it takes time, is expensive ($2,500 to $3,000 in attorney's, doctor's and court expenses in Pennsylvania) causes court reporting requirements, and requires court approval for certain transactions. The actual court procedures can be difficult and uncomfortable. In the court proceeding, mom typically hires an attorney and doctor who puts on evidence to prove that dad is incapacitated. The doctor runs through a series of questions about dad's physical and mental capacity and abilities for everything from reading to toileting. Then dad's attorney presents evidence that dad is all right and the court makes a decision. It is an ugly proceeding.

Sometimes, especially for someone who is single, the person appointed as guardian isn't necessarily the person you would choose to make financial and medical decisions for you but the loud-mouthed, busybody relative who yells the loudest and gets to the courthouse first. Remember, if you do not pick someone to make decisions for you, the court will.

Typically the person who is appointed guardian has to

..port no less than annually how many times they visit the incompetent, any doctors visits and where every penny is invested and spent. The guardian may also have to obtain specific court approval for certain transactions to make sure they are in the incapacitated person's best interest. In many states, when the incapacitated person passes, you have to make a final accounting of all visits and care and where every penny was invested and spent from the beginning of the guardianship until death.

This can be overwhelming for the guardian. This is especially true if the guardianship had been in place for a long time. For example, we represented a client who passed with a guardianship that had been in place for eight years. The incapacitated person also had several rentals that the guardian managed for many years. The final accounting to the court had to illustrate where every penny went for over eight years. Needless to say, this created a lot of work, accounting fees and legal expenses for the estate. **When we closed the file, our file was over eight inches thick! If a proper Power of Attorney had been in place and used, all the above court requirements could have been avoided.**

If dad in the above example had executed a proper Financial Power of Attorney, then mom would have had the legal authority to sign dad's name, sell the house and manage all the financial affairs for herself and her husband without unnecessary court involvement and unnecessary legal fees.

The format for a Financial Power of Attorney differs from state to state. Pennsylvania most recently changed its Financial Power of Attorney requirements in 2000, which required certain notices and disclosures be added. Pennsylvania Financial Powers of Attorney also can become too old. Meaning that if your Power of Attorney is older, a bank or financial institution may not accept it. Therefore, if you have a Power of Attorney that was signed ten years ago, and you still have capacity, you can avoid problems by executing a new Power of Attorney.

There are other concerns with Financial Powers of Attorney as well. Not only can Powers of Attorney not work, become old or stale, but the actual words of the Power of Attorney can also render it ineffective. For example, a Power of Attorney may allow your agent only to make "limited" gifts. This means gifts of $13,000 or less. This may sound good and many attorneys recommend Powers of Attorney that only allow limited gifts so that your agent cannot give all your stuff away if you become incapacitated. However, the problem is that sometimes we need to make gifts larger than $13,000 for asset protection purposes. To illustrate, assume dad is in a nursing home and is incapacitated. Mom is healthy and living at home. For as long as mom can live in their $200,000 home, it is protected from being used to pay for nursing home care. As do most couples, mom and dad hold title to the property jointly. Therefore, if mom predeceases dad, dad would inherit the house and the house would be used to pay for dad's long-term care (or the state would recover all the equity in the house).

The technique we use to protect the house in case mom passes first, is to have dad gift his one-half interest in the house to mom, and for mom to disinherit dad so that if mom predeceases dad, most if not all of the value of the house would go to mom and dad's beneficiaries and not to pay for dad's nursing care.

But if dad is incapacitated and has a Power of Attorney that only permits limited gifts, we have a problem. Since the house is worth $200,000, for dad to gift his one-half interest to mom to protect it, a gift of $100,000 would be required. If the power of attorney only authorizes "limited" gifts of $13,000 or less, the gift cannot be made and the house is unnecessarily at risk for going to pay for dad's long-term care.

By the way, in case you are wondering, I can't tell you how often we have seen the healthy caregiver, "the at-home spouse" predecease the ill spouse.

So re-read your Power of Attorney or have an attorney review the gifting power in your Financial Power of Attorney. The problem with unlimited gifting power is that your agent could gift away, i.e., steal, all your stuff. You must be able to trust the person you name as your agent in your Power of Attorney.

A colleague of ours was discussing this at a seminar, and a woman in the front row turned white as a ghost. But about ten minutes later, she was smiling from ear to ear. After the seminar, he wondered what brilliant thing he said that caused this reaction, so he approached her and asked why she had looked scared at one point in the seminar and happy just a few minutes later. She replied that she and her husband were having marital problems, "So when you said my husband, who is my Financial Power of Attorney, could take everything, I became scared that he could take all my assets. But after a few minutes, I remembered that I am his agent on his Financial Power of Attorney and since he is not here tonight, he does not realize that he can take my assets but I know I can take his."

To make sure someone can't use your Financial Power of Attorney until you are incapacitated, some attorneys use what is called a "two doctor standard," meaning that when two doctors put in writing that you are incapacitated, then you are incapacitated. Only then can my Financial Power of Attorney make a decision for me. This is called a "springing" power of Attorney because it only "springs" to life when two doctors say you are incapacitated.

This sounds like a good answer to a Power of Attorney only taking over while you still have capacity but then the HIPAA (Health Insurance Portability and Accountability Act) came along. The idea behind the law is to keep your health information private. This seems like a good idea, but if you have ever tried to call your spouse's health insurer or had to fill out a form at the doctor's office, you have dealt with some of the difficulties created by HIPAA.

If you have capacity when you enter a hospital, you can sign a HIPAA release that authorizes to whom the doctor can talk to on your behalf. **But what if you enter the hospital unconscious and cannot sign a HIPAA release?** The reason you have to sign a release is because a doctor and/or hospital are both civilly and criminally liable if they release your medical information to the wrong person. This makes doctors very cautious about putting anything about your medical condition in writing.

So if you have a Financial Power of Attorney that is only effective when two doctors put in writing that you are incapacitated and since doctors are unwilling to put in writing that you are incapacitated, your Power of Attorney is useless. Instead, we no longer prepare two-doctor standard "springing" Financial Powers of Attorney. We only recommend Powers of Attorney that are immediately effective upon signing to avoid this problem.

A few years ago, we did have a client who insisted on a two-doctor standard springing Financial Power of Attorney. We recommended that she not do it, but she insisted. Since she was the client and was paying the bill, we complied. She stated that she hadn't seen a doctor in over 50 years and she was going to manage her own affairs as long as she could.

Ironically, a few months after we signed her documents, she suffered a massive stroke, which left her in a coma, brain dead and on her deathbed. One of the additional problems was that she was the caregiver for her husband who was suffering from late stage Alzheimer's. In spite of her clear incapacity, it took her son almost three weeks to get two doctors to put in writing that she was incapacitated.

During the three weeks, the son had no control over mom's accounts and could not pay bills or otherwise take care of mom or dad's financial affairs. The lesson is that you should have your Power of Attorney reviewed to make sure it can speak for you if you can't speak for yourself. **If the Power of Attorney cannot speak for you when you cannot speak for yourself, it is not worth the paper it is printed on.**

Medical Power of Attorney and Living Will

The next document everyone should have in place is a Medical Power of Attorney and a Living Will directive. This document allows someone to make medical decisions for you if you cannot speak for yourself. The Living Will directive is the section where you can let your doctor and family know how you feel about end-of-life medical decisions such as the introduction and continuation of life support that only prolongs the process of dying.

In Pennsylvania, this document was updated and improved effective January 2007. If you are a Pennsylvania resident, consider updating your combined Medical Power of Attorney and Living Will directive. You need to have your current document reviewed and the updates clarified to you because the new form is much better than the old form.

However, if you have the old form, don't worry, the new law specifically states that the old form is still effective and binding.

The Living Will is not a perfect document, but it is the only way to let your doctors and family know your feelings as to end-of-life decisions. If you do not have your wishes in writing, legally the doctors and hospitals have to attach you to machines.

I sometimes talk to clients who say, "I don't want a Living Will, I want nothing done to prolong dying if no hope is left." Conversely, I have other clients who say, "I don't want a Living Will because I want the doctor and hospital to do everything possible to prolong my life." **My response is that no matter whether you want doctors to do nothing to continue your life or to do everything to continue your life, put it in writing so the doctors and your family know what to do.**

The most important thing a Living Will accomplishes is to let your family know what you want. I have had numerous calls from children of clients calling to thank me for putting a Living Will in place so that when the time came, they knew exactly what the parent wanted. This goes a long way to alleviate any guilt for the family because they are just carrying out their parent's wishes.

What types of estate plans are available?

1. No Plan. If you do not have a plan in place, guess who

has a plan for you? As you guessed, the Internal Revenue Service and your state do. **If you die with no Will, you are considered to have passed "intestate." When someone dies intestate, the IRS, state law and the court will decide who your beneficiaries are and who is in charge through the probate system or court process.** Do you really think the IRS has the best interest of you and your family at heart? The plan the IRS and your state have for you and your assets may be completely different than what you want to occur. **Do you *really* want the IRS and the state to write your estate plan?**

All your assets may not go to your surviving spouse. The first problem with dying intestate is that any of your relatives have standing to be appointed by the court as administrator of your estate. This means that your busybody spendthrift relative rather than your most trusted relative could manage your estate. Any plan is better than no plan. **We call this the "I hate you plan." Meaning, "I don't love you enough to clean up my own mess and you have to clean it up for me."**

2. Will. A Will is the most common of estate plans. It is a legal written document that names your beneficiaries and who gets what and when. It also names who is going to be in charge of your estate, the executor (male) or executrix (female). At a minimum, everyone should at least have in place a Will, Power of Attorney for Finance, Power of Attorney for Healthcare and a Living Will declaration.

There are several drawbacks to a Will. First of all, a Will guarantees that your estate will go through probate. **To clarify, a Will does not avoid probate. In fact it guarantees that your estate will go through probate, a court process that takes time, costs money and makes your estate a public record.**

In addition, a Will does not control the distribution of jointly held assets, nor does it control assets with a beneficiary designation such as IRA's, annuities and life insurance policies. So even if your Will states that everything goes to your spouse, if the beneficiary designation says the life insurance policy's proceeds go to your mom, the policy will go to your mom.

3. Joint Ownership. There are several types of joint ownership. The most common is Joint Tenancy With The Right of Survivorship or Tenancy By The Entireties. Most spouses own their home in this manner. This allows the property to transfer automatically to the survivor by operation of law and without going through probate at the death of the first spouse. The surviving tenant automatically owns the property at the passing of the joint tenant. This avoids probate on the death of the initial joint tenant but just delays it until the surviving joint tenant passes away. **So joint tenancy does not avoid probate. It just postpones it.**

Tenancy In Common is when you own the property with someone else but with no right of survivorship. When any co-owner passes away, the assets will not automatically

28

transfer to the survivor but instead passes according to the Will of the deceased. This court process is called probate. Assets held by Tenancy In Common will be subject to probate because the assets need to pass through the estate of the deceased tenant. There are potential problems with Joint Ownership. For example, Bob and Sue have a lovely home and are raising three kids. Unexpectedly, Sue passes away. The kids grow up and move away.

Then Bob meets and falls in love with Sylvia and marries her. After a few years, Sylvia's name is added to the deed. Then Bob dies. Since Sylvia was the joint tenant, ownership of the home went directly to her. But what happened to Bob's kids? Sadly, they did not get the house.

What if Bob had a Will that said the house goes to his kids? Then who gets the house? Sylvia still gets the house because a Will does not control assets held in Joint Ownership With The Right Of Survivorship. This type of situation is called "unintentional disinheritance" and is not unusual. With people living longer and second marriages becoming more common, this issue occurs all too frequently.

4. Beneficiary Designations. Another way to transfer assets at death is by beneficiary designation. When you set up accounts such as IRA's, retirement plans, annuities and insurance policies, the applications ask you to name beneficiaries who will receive the proceeds upon your death. Beneficiaries' only have to fill out a simple form and present a death certificate to take possession of the asset, since these accounts avoid probate. **A major drawback is that you have to keep your beneficiary designations current.**

For example, we had a client who had a life insurance policy for 35 years but had only been married for 30 years. When we reviewed the policy, we asked the client the name of the beneficiary on the policy. The client responded, "My wife, of course."

The beneficiary was not his wife. Can you guess who the beneficiary was? Yes, his mom. The next sound we heard was a thud under the dining room table. It was his wife, kicking him in the shins. Since mom was in a nursing home, it would have been a disaster had she received the insurance proceeds.

We had a similar situation with a $6000 life insurance policy. In that instance, the owner of the policy named his mother a beneficiary in 1959. The client passed in 2003 but his mom had passed in 1981. He never updated or checked his beneficiary designation. We were retained to help his surviving beneficiaries make a claim on the policy. This cost thousands of dollars and took a lot of time. If he had simply updated his beneficiaries, all the time and expense could have been avoided.

In his defense, probably 60-70% of the beneficiary designations that we review are incomplete or incorrect. Many have a primary beneficiary but not a secondary beneficiary. Some designations are outdated, and some name minors as beneficiaries. Sometimes people simply designate "my estate" as the beneficiary. This is the worst thing possible because again, an asset that would have avoided probate and quickly gone to a beneficiary, goes through probate causing delay and costing money.

If you have not recently checked your beneficiary designations, call the company holding the asset and/or policy and ask who are the primary and contingent beneficiaries. You may be surprised by the results. (If you are lucky, you won't get kicked under the table.)

There are also income tax advantages with an IRA that requires the designation of proper beneficiaries in order to be tax efficient. Generally, under the old IRS code, when someone inherited an IRA, the beneficiary had to claim the income in one lump sum or over five (5) years, at best. This means that if the beneficiary was in a 30% tax bracket (federal and state) and inherited $100,000 from an IRA, the net proceeds, after income tax, would only be $70,000.

Under the new Internal Revenue Service Code, the beneficiary can stretch withdrawing the money from an IRA over the beneficiary's life expectancy. For example, in accordance with his life expectancy, a beneficiary may only be required to withdraw 1% of the IRA per year. In the above example, this would allow the beneficiary to only withdraw 1% or $1,000 from the $100,000 IRA. The beneficiary would only pay income taxes on the $1,000 that was withdrawn or about $300, and the balance of the IRA, $99,000, could continue to grown tax deferred. The problem is that in order to "stretch out" the withdrawals over the life expectancy of the beneficiary, the beneficiary has to be properly designated as a beneficiary in accordance with the requirements of the Internal Revenue Service Code. If the requirements are not met, the stretch is lost and that entire IRA is subject to tax in one lump sum over five (5) years. This causes grave income tax consequences and can turn a $100,000 IRA into $70,000 overnight. Therefore, it is critical to make sure you have properly designated primary and secondary beneficiaries on your IRA.

5. *Gifting.* You can give away a lot of money in a short period of time to remove the asset out of your estate and avoid probate. **The problem is, once you give it away, you might not be able to get it back.** We need to clear up a common misconception. Most people (and, unfortunately, a lot of financial advisors) believe that you can only give $13,000 away per person, per year. You can actually not only give away $13,000 per person, per year but over that you can give $1,000,000 away during your lifetime. If you are married, you and your wife can gift $13,000 each year or $26,000 per person per year. All these gifts can be made without payment of gift taxes. (The amount over $13,000 has to be reported to the IRS on a gift tax return and reduces your lifetime unused credit but no gift taxes would be due up to $1,000,000.)

For example, if a widow gave $100,000 to her child, the first $13,000 would not have to be reported, but the $87,000 over the $13,000 would be reported to the IRS. The result is the widow's ability to give away $1,000,000 over her lifeti.... would be reduced by $87,000 to $911,000 over the balance of her lifetime. Therefore, the widow would be limited to gifting $911,000 over the remainder of her lifetime.

The gift of $13,000 is tax-free for both the person who makes the gift and the person who receives the gift. The recipient does not have to report or otherwise pay taxes on the gifted amount. Therefore, in the above example, the widow's child who received the $100,000 would not have to report the $100,000 as income. The only taxes due would be on the interest or earnings of the $100,000 after the date of the gift.

Therefore, you can give away a lot of money in a short period of time without income tax consequences. However, although it is easy to give stuff away, a lot of times it is much harder to get the stuff back if you need it.

Another problem with gifting away assets is that you might be creating a tax problem for the recipient. For example, suppose Bob bought his home in 1955 for $20,000 and today it's worth $150,000. He gives the house to his son Tom by selling it for $1.00.

Tom then sells the property for $150,000. Because Bob transferred the property to Tom while Bob was living, the house keeps Bob's old cost basis of $20,000. Remember that's what Bob paid for it. That means Tom now has a $130,000 gain on the sale. Under current law, he will have to pay approximately $19,500 in capital gains tax. This is true not only for real estate but also for any gift of any appreciated asset such as stock.

This problem could have been avoided if Tom had inherited the property at Bob's passing. If Tom inherits the house at Bob's death, Tom receives a "stepped up" basis to the fair market value of the property at the time of Tom's death. So now when Tom sells the property, there is no capital gain. By not gifting the house, Tom saves $19,500 in capital gains taxes.

The other problem with making gifts is that any gift over $500 can cause a penalty period where you cannot apply for Medicaid. This topic will be more fully discussed later but if you are going to make a gift, you have to understand all the tax and Medicaid penalty issues that may be involved. Thus, before making any sizable gift, please talk to your accountant and attorney. **Just because you are allowed to make a gift does not mean that you won't be penalized for the gift!**

CHAPTER 4
WHAT IS PROBATE?

Before we can talk about how a Revocable Living Trust in some cases can be a valuable estate planning tool and avoid probate, we must first clarify what probate is and what probate is not. Some people, mainly probate attorneys and uninformed financial advisors, say that probate is "no big deal" and that "there is no reason to avoid it."

Conversely, a handful of misinformed attorneys and financial advisors claim that probate is the worst creation ever unleashed on civilized man. Both of the groups are liars, but I am going to discuss only the facts about probate.

Probate is a legal process by which a court identifies assets, identifies who is in charge, and recognizes creditors and identifies beneficiaries. If there is a Will, the court will validate the Will and settle any disputes or Will contests. If there is no Will, the court will determine who is in charge and determine who are the beneficiaries. **If a person dies with any assets in his or her name but with no beneficiary named, the estate will go through probate.**

Just to clarify: A Will does not avoid probate. In fact, a Will is a one-way ticket to the probate process. If you have a Will, probate is the only way to transfer property after you die if the asset is only in your name with no beneficiaries.

Why does probate exist? Let me use this example to

illustrate why probate exists. Assume grandma, a widow, dies owning a house. None of her children or grandchildren wants or need the house, so the family decides to sell it.

Lo and behold, the first person to walk in the house offers to buy the house for the asking price, with cash. A few weeks later, there is a closing meeting to sell the house at an attorney's office. At the closing, a deed lays on the attorney's conference room table. What is the problem with the deed at closing? Obviously, grandma can't sign the deed. So the main reason probate exists is because dead people cannot sign their names. Essentially, the purpose of the probate court is to appoint someone who is authorized to sign for the deceased person.

(By the way, if you thought the person who held grandma's Financial Power of Attorney could sign her name, remember, that a Power of Attorney stops at death. Therefore, after grandma died, grandma's Power of Attorney stopped and her agent no longer had authority to sign her name and therefore, could not sign the deed).

The other reason probate exists is to make sure creditors are paid. But the truth is, unless the estate is bankrupt, most creditors do not use the probate process to get paid when someone dies. Typically, the creditors send the bills, the person in charge of the estate determines if the debt is legitimate and pays the legitimate bills. AARP's report on probate in 1990 determined that even then, only about 5% of creditors used the probate process to get paid. The percentage would be much less now.

To understand probate, you have to put probate into perspective. The probate process is basically the same today as it was 100 years ago. I would bet that a probate attorney from 1909 could probate an estate today. Keep in mind that 100 years ago, when we were an agrarian society, the guy at the feed store who gave farmer Bob credit might not find out that farmer Bob died for months. Probate was created to make sure the guy at the feed store received notice of farmer Bob's death and that he got paid.

I know what you may be thinking, "I do not have unpaid creditors, so why should my estate go though probate?" *That is exactly the point. Why should your family go though probate if they do not have to?*

Probate varies from state to state. Some states have a relatively simple process and some are more complex. In Pennsylvania, if someone dies with a Will or with no Will and has an asset in only their name with no beneficiary named, the estate will go through probate.

In Pennsylvania, the probate process for a person who prepared a Will is essentially as follows: Typically, the original Will and a certified death certificate are given to an attorney who prepares a petition to the court to have the court appoint an executor of the estate. The executor is the person in charge of wrapping up the affairs of the decedent, paying bills and taxes, and distributing assets to the beneficiaries. The executor takes the original Will, a certified death certificate and the petition to the Register of Wills office in the county where the decedent passed away as a resident. A fee is paid and the Register decides whether to admit the Will to probate or not.

If the Will is not "self-proving," the witnesses to the Will have to approve or sign an affidavit authenticating the decedent's signature or present a signed affidavit of unavailability that has to be presented explaining why the witnesses cannot attend (i.e., the witnesses are dead or moved to Florida).

If the Will and petition are accepted, the Register's representative makes the executor/executrix swear an oath essentially that they will carry out their duties and comply with all applicable laws.

Then a notice has to be given to the decedent's intestate heirs **whether they are beneficiaries or not. We call this the "shake the nuts out of the tree" notice. The notice goes to your intestate heirs whether or not they are beneficiaries. The notice basically tells them they may or may not be a beneficiary of the decedent's estate but that if they do not act, their right to contest the estate will expire.**

After a notice is sent to the intestate beneficiaries, then a certification of the sending of the notice is filed with the court.

Next the estate is advertised in the local legal journal and a local paper of general circulation for a period of three consecutive weeks.

Next an inventory of the probatable assets of the estate is prepared and filed with the court. The inventory is just what it sounds like, a list of all the value of probatable assets as of the date of death.

The executor then prepares or has prepared a Commonwealth of Pennsylvania inheritance tax return. The return is due and taxes paid within nine (9) months of the death of the decedent. However, if the return is filed and taxes paid within 90 days of death, a credit of 5% of the tax due is given on the amount of taxes due. If you have enough liquidity (i.e., not all real estate) in the estate, usually, it is best to take advantage of the discount period.

The rate of inheritance tax is 0% to spouses, 4.5% to lineal heirs (children, stepchildren, grandchild, parents or grandparents) 12% to siblings and 15% to everyone else.

With some limited exceptions, the only asset not subject to Pennsylvania inheritance tax after deducting for estate-related and funeral expenses and debts of the decedent is life insurance. Pennsylvania typically takes 6 to 12 weeks to determine whether the state accepts the return as filed or if they have questions, challenges or the need for additional information.

After the state approves the return, either the family receives an informal accounting and signs a family settlement agreement that typically is filed with the court or the court is petitioned and a formal accounting of the estate is filed with the court. Sixty days ahead of time, the accounting and notice is filed with the court and given to the beneficiaries. After 60 days, the attorney presents the petition to the court and the court typically asks the attorney if all bills and taxes are paid (and sometimes asks if a monument has been erected and paid for) to which the attorney better respond, "Yes." If any beneficiary has a challenge to the administrator of the estate, the challenge can be raised at the accounting.

If no one brings a claim, the judge signs off on the accounting. If no one appeals after 30 days, the judge signs off on the estate and the administration is complete. At that point, another notice is filed with the court to tell the court that the administration of the estate is complete, and finally, the probating of the Will is completed. As you can see, there is a lot of "hurry up and wait" built into the process.

There are three main reasons to avoid probate: Time, Publicity and Attorney's Fees.

1. Time. The first reason to avoid probate is the time it takes to administer the estate. We tell clients to expect about a year for the complete probate of an estate. A Pennsylvania probate attorney was quoted in the Allegheny County Legal Journal as stating that a simple estate takes 9 to 12 months to administrate and a typical estate takes 12 to 15 months. We tell our clients to expect 12 months and we look like heroes if it only takes 9 months and snails if it ends up taking 15 months. Nationwide, AARP conducted a survey, which showed the nationwide time for probate to be about 2 years.

A year is a long time to administer an estate. If your estate is not organized, if no Will or Trust is in place, or if there are family issues, it can take even longer.

This time can be especially troublesome if the person you name as executor lives out of state. Essentially the executor is tied into a far away court system for 9 to 15 months.

2. Publicity. Most people keep their Will in a safe or in a safety deposit box because it is a private document. In addition, most people are also private about how much they make, the size of their investments and what their expenses are. However, when your estate goes through probate, your Will and all of your financial affairs are a public record. In fact, the advertising of the estate in the newspaper and the 5.6 Notice encourages the entire community, including your nosy neighbors or disgruntled heirs, to make a claim against your estate.

Because probate is a public record, anyone can find out the contents of your Will, the size of your estate, your expenses, your social security number, the names and addresses of your beneficiaries, and what they are going to receive. As you can imagine, people can easily take advantage of this knowledge.

If you want, go to the Register of Wills or Clerk of Courts Office and ask to look at old probate estates to see the detail involved, especially in a case with a formal inventory or a family settlement agreement. Ask to see files that are over two years old, since the administration of these files should be completed. (If you look at files less than two years old, the administration probably would not be complete and you may not see a completely probated estate). You will be surprised at the information you will see.

3. Attorney's Fees. The third reason to avoid probate is due to the attorney's fees. Attorneys are entitled to a "reasonable fee" for probating an estate. In some states the law sets the fees. In other states, the fees have to be "reasonable." In Pennsylvania, attorneys are entitled to a "reasonable fee" for probating an estate. A "reasonable fee" is typically based on the *Johnson Estate Case.* According to the case, a "reasonable fee" for a typical estate is 3% to 7% of the gross estate depending on the size of the estate. I have enclosed a copy of the fee schedule from the *Johnson Estate Case* on the next page for your reference. The case illustrates that a reasonable fee on a $200,000 gross probated estate is $9,750. Do you want an attorney to be a $9,750 "beneficiary" of your hard earned $200,000 estate?

Please note that this fee is on the gross probatable estate not the net estate. Therefore, if you own a $350,000 home but have a $200,000 mortgage, for purposes of calculating attorney's fees, you have a gross probatable estate of $350,000. Once an estate goes to probate, the attorney also is entitled to 1% of the non-probatable estate. So if you have a $300,000 IRA and a $300,000 life insurance policy, the attorney is also entitled to 1% of the proceeds from these assets as a reasonable fee even though the assets did not go through probate and went directly to the hopefully properly named beneficiaries. You can calculate what it would cost to probate your estate using the fee schedule below:

COMMISSIONS

						Per Col.	Per Total
	$	0.01	To $	100,000.00	5%	5,000.00	5,000.00
Executor or	$	100,000.01	To $	200,000.00	4%	4,000.00	9,000.00
Administrator	$	200,000.01	To $	1,000,000.00	3%	24,000.00	33,000.00
	$	1,000,000.01	To $	2,000,000.00	2%	20,000.00	53,000.00
	$	2,000,000.01	To $	3,000,000.00	1½ %	15,000.00	68,000.00
	$	3,000,000.01	To $	4,000,000.00	1	10,000.00	78,000.00
	$	4,000,000.01	To $	5,000,000.00	½ %	5,000.00	83,000.00

	1% Joint Accounts 3% Real Estate Converted with Aid of Broker	1% P.O.D. Bonds 5% Real Estate: Non-Converted	1% Trust Funds 1% Real Estate: Specific Devise

						Per Col.	Per Total
	$	0.01	To $	25,000.00	7%	1,750.00	1,750.00
Attorney	$	25,000.01	To $	50,000.00	6%	1,500.00	3,250.00
	$	50,000.01	To $	100,000.00	5%	2,500.00	5,750.00
	$	100,000.01	To $	200,000.00	4%	4,000.00	9,750.00
	$	200,000.00	To $	1,000,000.00	3 %	24,000.00	33,750.00
	$	1,000,000.00	To $	2,000,000.00	2%	20,000.00	53,750.00
	$	2,000,000.00	To $	3,000,000.00	1½ %	15,000.00	68,7500.00
	$	3,000,000.00	To $	4,000,000.00	1%	10,000.00	78,750.00
	$	4,000,000.00	To $	5,000,000.00	½ %	5,000.00	83,750.00

½% Regular Commission P.O.D. Bonds and Trust Funds
1% Non-Probate Assets up to 3 ½ % Transfer

Joint Accounts
1% Non-Probate Assets
3½ % Assets Which are Taxable at One Half Value
Joint Accounts Fully Taxable: Full Commission

By the way, the worst thing you can do is make "My Estate" the beneficiary of retirement plans, an IRA, annuities, and/or life insurance because this makes a potentially probate avoided asset fully probatable and subject to a full attorney's fee. The assets that typically avoid probate are retirement plans, an IRA, annuities and life insurance. The rest of your assets go through probate. The typical ones are real estate, most bank accounts, bonds, most non-IRA brokerage accounts, US Savings Bonds, timeshares and stock. Some attorneys charge for probate by the hour but that amount can turn out to be even more than a flat percentage rate.

For those who own property in more than one state, even timeshares, the estate can go through multiple probates in each state involved. This means additional attorneys in each state involved. So if you have a home in Pennsylvania and a condo in Florida, your estate would not only go through probate here, but you would also have an ancillary probate in Florida. Two probates are not better than one. Two sets of attorney's fees are not better than one.

We once probated an estate and the deceased had a timeshare on Hilton Head Island, South Carolina. The timeshare was worth about $12,000 at the time. We hired a South Carolina attorney to handle the probate of the timeshare. The South Carolina attorney charged, including fees and expenses, about $5,000.

You will notice that I did not mention court costs. The court costs make up only a small amount of probate expenses.

On a $200,000 probatable estate, the actual court costs, filing fees and advertising expenses would only be about $1,000 at most. However, the attorney's fees on a $300,000 estate would be about $12,000.

As you can see, these fees and expenses can add up to a substantial portion of your estate. Every dollar paid in attorney's fees is a dollar your heirs do not receive. The saddest part is that heirs end up selling assets just to pay the fees and taxes.

Can probate be avoided? Yes! Probate can be avoided through the use of a properly funded Revocable Living Trust.

CHAPTER 5
WHAT IS A REVOCABLE LIVING TRUST?

The best way to explain a Trust is by returning to our story of the widow grandma who passed away. Remember when grandma died owning a house and the children decided to sell the house? The problem we had with the deed at closing on the sale of the house was that grandma passed away, and therefore, could not sign the deed. Since grandma could not sign the deed, we had to probate grandma's Will so the court could give someone else the authority to sign grandma's name on the deed.

A Trust is, simply, a contract that appoints someone to sign your name if you died (or became incapacitated). In our example, if grandma had a Trust, the terms of the Trust (the contract) would designate who had the authority to sign grandma's name after she died. Since the Trust, which serves as the contract, gave the authority to someone to sign grandma's name, the estate would not have to be probated. Since the estate did not have to be probated, this saved the heirs time and money while keeping the distribution of the estate as private as possible.

In order for the Trust to work, the assets have to be funded into the Trust. This is critical and all too often overlooked, but it is a process we help our clients with every step of the way. If you have another attorney or a financial planner assist

46

you with your Trust, make sure they fund the Trust, especially filing any deeds. Deeds in Pennsylvania have to be filed within ninety (90) days of signing or the estate will have to be probated to clear title on the deed. If you have a Trust without a deed filed in Pennsylvania, make immediate arrangements to have a new deed prepared and filed.

There are several types of Trusts. The type we are talking about now is a Revocable Living Trust. It is called a Living Trust because it is created and funded while you are alive. This is opposed to a Testamentary Trust which is created now but only funded at your death through a Will and is typically funded through the probate process.

A Trust is a contract that continues after you die. It is a separate legal entity that survives you. You simply transfer assets to your Trust. My Trust is the Shields Family Revocable Living Trust. Most importantly, while you are alive and able, you control the assets of the Trust. The IRS actually says that since you are still in control of your assets in a Revocable Living Trust, the Trust is still identified by your social security number and you still pay the same federal income taxes.

Many people are under the misconception that if they put their assets in a Revocable Living Trust that someone else, such as a bank's Trust department or their children are immediately in control of their assets. **Let me reiterate that with a Revocable Living Trust, as long as you are alive and able, you maintain complete control of all of your**

assets.

If you pass away or if you become incapacitated, only then does someone else manage your assets, typically a child, relative or trusted friend. For the management of assets, a Trust can be better than a Power of Attorney for two reasons. First, Powers of Attorney become stale. Some banks will not accept a Power of Attorney or will want a recertification of the Power of Attorney if it is over six (6) months old. Conversely, since a Revocable Living Trust is a contract, it never becomes stale. Furthermore, since the US Constitution protects our right to enter into contracts, this right to contract can never be taken away.

The other reason a Trust is better than a Power of Attorney is that when you die, the Power of Attorney stops working. Since a Trust is a contract, it keeps working after you pass away and your family can continue to manage your affairs.

I cannot tell you how many times I have had the child of a parent added to a bank account as a Power of Attorney so they could sign checks for the parent. To the child's dismay, when the parent passes away, the Power of Attorney can no longer be used. The account is frozen and the estate has to be probated, prior to any more banking being allowed. A Trust would avoid all of these problems. In fact, one way to think of a Trust is to think of it as a Power of Attorney that survives death.

So what happens with a Trust is as follows: Number one, as long as you are alive and able, you retain control of your assets just as you always have; Number two, if you become incapacitated, the assets are managed by someone you choose in the manner you specify; Number three, at your passing, the assets are again managed by the person you chose, the bills and taxes will be paid and then the remaining assets will be distributed directly to your beneficiaries per your instructions in the Trust.

Previously we discussed why assets such as annuities and life insurance proceeds go directly to your beneficiaries at your death. For example, I have a contract with a life insurance company that says if I pay them money, when I die, after they receive a death certificate, they pay my wife her money. This works because it is a contract with beneficiaries. Think of a Trust as a same thing. It allows you to enter into a contract with beneficiaries with assets such as real estate where you typically cannot name beneficiaries.

The advantages to the Revocable Living Trust are as follows:

1. Keeps Your Affairs as Private as Possible

Because there is no probate, your Will and Trust is not filed as a public record, no estate has to be advertised and no inventory has to be filed.

2. Saves Time

The Trust greatly reduces the time it takes to settle the estate. Your successor trustee, the person who takes over when you pass away, can be in charge as soon as he or she obtains death certificates. The estate can be settled as quickly or as slowly as the successor trustee desires. Typically, we can settle a properly funded Revocable Living Trust in 12 to 15 weeks rather than a probate, which takes 12 to 15 months.

3. Avoids Court Intervention

When you avoid probate, you avoid court. No one likes going to court. Probate court is especially inconvenient if the person in charge lives out of state.

4. Greatly Reduces Attorney Fees

As attorneys, we typically charge a reasonable fee of 3% to 7% of the gross estate in Pennsylvania of an average estate. While a Trust is more expensive to set up (anywhere from $2,000 to $3,000 for a simple Trust) it is much less expensive to settle. (Maybe 1% of the gross estate in attorney's fees.) We typically charge $1,000 to settle a properly funded Trust that we set up unless there is a Federal Estate Tax return required (currently for estates over $3,500,000) and therefore, an additional fee is charged.

Please note, that while a Revocable Living Trust in Pennsylvania avoids probate, reduces attorneys fees, avoids a second probate in other states where you own property and keeps affairs private, **it does not protect assets from long-term care (except in certain limited cases) and does not avoid Pennsylvania's state inheritance tax.** Some financial planners frequently imply that a Revocable Living Trust can protect assets from long-term care and/or avoid Pennsylvania's inheritance tax. **This is a lie.** Since you are in control of a Revocable Living Trust, the assets are still yours and under your control, therefore, if you need long-term care, the assets must be used or spent down for your care.

In addition, whether you die intestate, have a Will or have a Trust or, if you die having more assets than liabilities, you owe Pennsylvania inheritance tax. I wish I had a nickel for every time I have had a prospective client tell me that a financial planner told him that a Revocable Living Trust reduces Pennsylvania inheritance tax.

A Revocable Living Trust can help to reduce Federal Estate Tax but before we discuss Federal Estate Tax I have to talk about the biggest enemy of proper estate planning in what will be the shortest chapter of this book.

CHAPTER 6
WHAT IS THE BIGGEST ENEMY OF PROPER ESTATE PLANNING?

PROCRASTINATION!

I could stop here but I can't. I have made too many emergency trips to the hospital (one time the anesthesiologist and I arrived at the same time at the bedside prior to open-heart surgery), too many trips to assisted living facilities, and too many trips to nursing homes. For you married couples, you decided to get married together, where you were going to live, what cars you bought, where the kids went to school, etc., so why not do your estate planning together as well?

I cannot tell you how many times I have visited a widow or widower who, when married, could make decisions at the snap of a finger. But, after losing a partner the survivor becomes overwhelmed and unable to make even a simple decision. Alone, the work doubled and he or she could no longer make decisions because the co-decision maker of 30, 40 or even 50 or more years is gone.

I'm sure you have seen these people as well. **I implore you to please do your planning together so you don't have to leave your spouse or your family to clean up your mess behind you. Preparing an estate plan is too important for you to procrastinate. Failure to plan is planning to fail. I would rather have a plan in place and not need it for years rather than need it and not have it in place.**

52

CHAPTER 7
FEDERAL ESTATE TAX REDUCTION

What is Federal Estate Tax and why should you care? In 2008 the Federal Estate Tax exemption was $2000,000. Currently in 2009, Federal Estate Tax only affects estates greater than $3,500,000. However, this amount will change. In 2010 there will be no Federal Estate Taxes and in 2011 the exemption is scheduled to drop to $1,000,000. With proper estate planning, you can reduce or eliminate Federal Estate Taxes.

The rate of tax is the issue. The maximum Federal Estate Tax on an estate can be anywhere from 37% to 55%, depending on the size of the estate and the year you die. Right now, there is no Federal Estate Tax for people with large estates who pass away in 2010. So the best year to die (from a tax standpoint) is 2010. **The problem with that plan is that you must be really dedicated to that plan, i.e., you have to be willing to die in 2010 for it to work!**

If you had $3,000,000 and had died in 2008 when the exemption was $2,000,000, the $2,000,000 would have been exempt from Federal Estate Tax and the $1,000,000 overage would have been subject to Federal Estate Tax. The effective rate of Federal Estate Tax on the $1,000,000 would have been about 46% of the $1,000,000 overage, and $460,000 would have gone to the IRS to pay for Federal Estate Taxes.

For married couples, we use an "AB" Trust to reduce Federal Estate Taxes. Every day I see clients who ask, "I heard about an AB Trust but how does it reduce taxes? What does the A stand for and what does the B stand for?" To answer their questions, I use the following example.

Suppose a husband and wife had $4,000,000 in 2008. If no planning had been done, when the husband died, his wife would have owned $4,000,000. If she had then also died in 2008, $2,000,000 would have been exempt from Federal Estate Tax but taxes would have been due on $2,000,000 and that would have resulted in approximately a $920,000 tax payment to Uncle Sam.

Each spouse had the right to protect $2,000,000. In the above example, if the wife had received all the proceeds from her husband, his exemption would have been forfeited and a large tax bill would have been the result.

However, what if a husband and wife had done some planning and had an AB Trust in place? What does "A" stand for and what does "B" stand for? I will tell you the answer and you will never forget it. "A" stands for "Above ground spouse" and "B" stands for, you got it "Below ground spouse."

Here's how it works. When the husband died, the wife kept her $2,000,000 in her "A" Trust. She also disclaimed $2,000,000 into a "B" Trust, which she could control and used generally for her health, education and welfare. The difference this time is that both spouses' exemptions were preserved. If the wife had passed away, the $2,000,000 in her "A" Trust was protected by her $2,000,000 exemption. But this time we had preserved the husband's $2,000,000 exemption so the $2,000,000 in the "B" is protected from Federal Estate Tax. Since $2,000,000 was protected from Federal Estate Tax by the wife's exemption in the A share and the husband's $2,000,000 was protected in the B share, their children would have inherited $4,000,000 federal estate tax free. This is a tax savings of $920,000 over the example where no planning was done.

CHAPTER 8
WHO SHOULD CONSIDER A
REVOCABLE LIVING TRUST?

Our general rule of thumb is that if your home in Pennsylvania or your probatable estate is worth at least $100,000 you should at least consider a Revocable Living Trust. The reason is that if you probate a $100,000 home, the attorney's fees and court costs for doing so would be approximately $5,000. If you paid $2,000 for a Revocable Living Trust and $1,000 to settle the Trust at your death, this would be a net savings to your family of $2,000. Strictly from a financial standpoint, in this example, a Revocable Living Trust makes sense. This does not even take into consideration the other benefits of a Revocable Living Trust and a proper estate plan.

Conversely, if your home or gross probatable estate was worth only $50,000, a Revocable Living Trust does not make financial sense. To probate a $50,000 estate would cost about $3,000 in attorney's fees and court costs. As a Trust would cost approximately $2,000 to establish and $1,000 to settle, the Revocable Trust would actually cost you more than probate. **This is why we disagree with those who say that everyone needs a Revocable Living Trust. The person with a $50,000 estate should be fine with a Will, Power of Attorney for Finance and Healthcare and a Living Will.**

A Revocable Living Trust plan is also especially

important for single people who have no legally recognized partner in the event of incapacity or death. Since they do not have a spouse to use an AB Trust, other planning techniques are required.

In addition, if you want to name a "significant other" as a beneficiary or manager of your estate should you become incapacitated or pass away, you need a written plan because most states do not recognize or give priority to non-relatives to be a beneficiary or serve as a court-appointed guardian of your estate.

Some other reasons to consider a Revocable Living Trust are as follows: if you own a second home or timeshare, especially if it is in a different state; if you want to pass your estate to your heirs with little delay or expense; if you want your affairs to be managed the way you direct if you become incapacitated or pass away; if you want your affairs to remain as private as possible; or if you have a second marriage.

As an aside, we often do planning for people in second marriages. The typical concern I hear when there is a second marriage and both spouses have children is "I want to take care of my spouse, but I want my assets to go to my children and she wants her assets to go to her children." Two individual Trusts can provide this protection because a Trust becomes irrevocable on the death of either spouse. This makes sure the Trust can't be changed after the death of a spouse. This way the deceased can make sure the spouse is provided for and also make sure that ultimately, the assets will go to the deceased's children.

The other common issue is the house. Frequently, prior to the marriage, each spouse owns his or her own home. The husband sells his house and moves into the wife's house but the house remains in the wife's name. The concern is that if the wife dies, what happens to the house? Do the wife's children kick the husband out?

In the wife's Trust, we can provide that the husband can live in the house for as long as it is his primary residence and he pays for taxes and utilities and regular maintenance. When he dies or the house is no longer his primary residence, the house goes to the wife's children. (Typically, we also add that if husband lives with a woman who is not a relative, his right to reside in the house lapses). This protects the surviving spouse from the other spouse's kids, and protects the kids from the surviving spouse.

As stated previously, AARP conducted a study on probate and called it a "cash cow" for attorneys. AARP proposed legislation that basically said that if a client asks for a Will, the attorney should not only discuss the Will and the cost to set up the Will, but the attorney should provide an estimate as to what it would cost to probate the estate. In addition, AARP recommended that the attorney should also discuss alternatives to probate such as a Trust, beneficiary configurations, and transfer on death accounts, etc.

Setting up a Will, while important, is relatively inexpensive. **If you ever ask an attorney to set up a Will,**

also ask what the lawyer will charge to settle the estate. Very often the lawyer will make an excuse to avoid answering the question. The lawyer will say, "I can't give you an estimate because it depends on too many factors, whether a beneficiary contests things or not or the size of the estate," etc. The attorney will use any excuse to avoid questions on fees because the attorney knows the fees will be very high and the client may object to it. Unfortunately when the grieving family comes to probate the estate, the client who hired the attorney can't complain about the fee.

Frequently the family just wants to settle the estate and get the inheritance as soon as possible so they will pay the lawyer's fee to expedite settling the estate.

A Trust is a little more work and expense up front, but saves a lot of time, work, and money for the beneficiaries. Like the old muffler commercial, "You can pay me now or you can pay me later."

I personally do not care whether a client chooses a Will or a Trust. The goal of this book is to educate the public about their alternatives and after they know the facts, then the consumer can make an educated decision. **What frustrates me is that many attorneys do not even explain to their client the estate planning options that are available to them.**

CHAPTER 9
WHAT IS "MEDICAID" AND WHY SHOULD I CARE?

Medicaid is a federal program that is implemented by the states. Medicaid typically pays for long-term skilled nursing care. Long-term skilled nursing care is expensive and the costs are skyrocketing. For example, in Pennsylvania, one month of skilled care costs over $7,000 per month, or $84,000 per year! I don't care how much money you have, $7,000 per month is a lot of money.

You should care about Medicaid because if you do not have a lot of money or long-term care insurance, *Medicaid is the only source we have to pay for long- term skilled care.*

In Pennsylvania, approximately 63% of people in skilled long-term care facilities have their bills paid by Medicaid. Persons on Medicaid ended up there in one of two ways. Either they spent all the money they had on care, had no money left and then qualified for Medicaid or they did some planning to protect assets (i.e., maybe for an at-home spouse) and qualified for Medicaid as soon as possible.

What is the difference between "Medicare" and "Medicaid?"
Medicare is a Healthcare program if we are 65 or older or are disabled. In general, Medicare, depending on the supplement can pay for just about all medical care as long

as one is improving, including up to a maximum 100 days of skilled long-term care.

But what happens if one does not or will not improve? What if someone has a degenerative disease such as Alzheimer's, MS, Parkinson's, Dementia, etc.? If you have one of these diseases, chances are that at some point in time, you will need skilled long-term care. Medicare will not pay for this care. On average, you will also live 8 to 12 years after diagnosis.

Medicaid will pay for this skilled care but you have to be broke to qualify for Medicaid. For example, if you are a single person in a Pennsylvania skilled care facility that accepts Medicaid, and you have $100,000 in the bank, you would have to spend your assets down to $8,000 or $2,400 in Pennsylvania prior to qualifying for Medicaid. (The amount you can keep varies depending on whether you are considered "high income or low income.")

There are basically seven tests to qualify for Medicaid.

- First of all, you have to be sick enough. This means you need skilled long-term care. Typically if someone is in a skilled care nursing home, they meet this test.

- Second you have to be 65 years of age or older or adjudicated as disabled if younger than 65.

- Third you have to be a US citizen.

- Fourth you have to be a resident of the state within which you are in a nursing home. If you are living in a Pennsylvania nursing home, you are considered to be a

61

Pennsylvania resident.

- Fifth, there are potentially some income limitations particularly if there is a married spouse residing in the family home.
- Sixth there are asset limitations on what the institutionalized spouse can keep and what a community or at-home healthy spouse can keep.
- Finally, and most importantly, you have to meet the asset and income requirements in a compliant manner. This means that you cannot give away all your money today and go to a nursing home tomorrow claiming you are now broke, and want to obtain Medicaid benefits.

If you pass all of the above tests and agree to give the nursing home your income, you qualify for Medicaid benefits. You get to keep a small monthly allowance. In Pennsylvania, you get to keep $45 per month of your income.

Medicaid is a good program. It pays for a lot of things.

- It pays for a semi-private room and board.
- It pays for all medicines, including co-pays.
- It pays for all health insurance premiums.
- It pays for any necessary physical therapy and pays for medically necessary odds and ends.

But there are some important limitations on what Medicaid pays that need to be understood. Medicaid does not pay for a private room or a private nurse. It does not pay for cable TV, phone service, haircuts, eyewear or dentures. In Pennsylvania, the $45.00 personal needs allowance is supposed to take care of all these expenses.

Maybe you think the above is not that big of a deal, however, for someone who has capacity but is in a nursing home due to a physical limitation, the phone and cable television provide a lifeline to the outside world and $45.00 per month will not pay for this.

The idea behind planning is to protect some of grandma's money to pay for the things she needs. If grandma is out of money, she is out of options. If grandma does not have money to pay for what she needs, who does? The kids? The grandkids?

Please note, if you have a loved one in a nursing home, the best thing you can do for them is to visit frequently, at irregular times. Invariably, a facility is going to be short-staffed. If the facility knows that your loved one may have someone showing up and the lady down the hall hasn't had a visitor in five years, who do you think is going to be cleaned and dressed first? Make sure you come during different shifts and get to know the staff.

How do you find good long-term skilled care? First of all, visit the facility twice. Visit once during regular hours and for the second time, visit during the second shift when the bosses aren't there and see if the facility still runs the same.

The "sandwich test" is one way to see if the facility is clean enough and smells good enough that you would feel comfortable eating a sandwich in the hallway.

The nurse's aide test is when you visit the facility and

observe the staff. Do not look for a doctor, because you will not find one. Do not look for nurses because they are too busy filling out paperwork. Look for the nurse's aides. The nurse's aides are really the ones who take care of the residents! Observe to see if the nurse's aides are attentive and relatively upbeat. Since they are caregivers, if the nurse's aides are attentive and upbeat, you are probably in a good facility.

By the way, the nurse's aides have no idea whether someone is a private payer or on Medicaid. As long as they get paid their hourly wage, they do not care where the money comes from. Therefore, whether or not you are private pay or Medicaid, you receive the same care from the nurse's aide.

The decision to move a family member or loved one into a nursing home is one of the most difficult decisions you can make. Perhaps the move is being made because the family member can no longer care for himself or herself or has a progressive disease like Alzheimer's or has had a stroke or heart attack. No matter the reason, those involved are almost always under great stress. At times like these, it's important that you pause, take a deep breath and understand that there are things you can do. Good information is available and you can make the right choices for you and your loved one.

Americans are living longer than ever before. At the turn of the 20th century, the average life expectancy was about 47 years. As we enter the 21st century, life expectancy has almost doubled. As a result, we face more challenges and transitions in our lives than those who came before us. One of the most difficult transitions people face is the change from independent living in his/her own home or apartment to living in a long-term care facility or "nursing home." There are many reasons why this transition is so difficult.

One reason is the loss of the home where the person lived for so many years with a lifetime of memories. Another is the loss of independence. Still another is the loss of the level of privacy we enjoy at home, since nursing home living is often shared with a roommate. Most people who make the decision to move to a nursing home do so during a time of great stress. Some have been hospitalized after a stroke, some have fallen and broken a hip, still others have progressive dementia, like Alzheimer's disease, and can no longer be cared for in their own homes. Whatever the reason, the spouse or relative who helps a person transition into a nursing home during a time of stress faces the immediate dilemma of how to find the right nursing home.

The task is no small one, and a huge sigh of relief can be heard when the right home is found and the loved one is moved into the nursing home. For many, the most difficult task is just beginning: How to cope with nursing home bills that may total $7,000 to $8,000 per month or more?

How to Pay for Nursing Home Care

One of the things that concern people most about nursing home care is how to pay for that care. There are basically four ways that you can pay the cost of a nursing home:

1. Long-Term Care Insurance. If you are fortunate enough to have this type of coverage, it may go a long way toward paying the cost of the nursing home. Unfortunately, long-term care insurance has only recently become popular and most people facing a nursing home stay do not have this coverage. In addition, many people either are not healthy enough to qualify for long-term insurance or it simply may be cost prohibitive.

2. Pay with Your Own Funds. This is the method many people are required to use at first. Quite simply, it means paying for the cost of a nursing home out of your own pocket. Unfortunately, with nursing home bills averaging between $7,000 and $8,000 per month in our area, few people can afford a long-term stay in a nursing home.

3. Medicare. This is the national health insurance program primarily for people 65 years of age and older, certain younger disabled people, and people with kidney failure. Medicare provides short-term assistance with nursing home costs, (20 to 100 days depending on your supplement) but only if you meet the strict qualification rules.

4. Medicaid. This is a federal and state funded and state administered medical benefit program which can pay for the cost of the nursing home if certain asset and income tests are met. Since the first two methods of private pay (i.e. using your own funds) and long-term care insurance are self-explanatory, our discussion will concentrate on Medicare and Medicaid.

66

What is Medicaid?

Medicaid is a benefit program, which is primarily funded by the federal government and administered by each state. Sometimes the rules can vary from state to state. One primary benefit of Medicaid is that, unlike Medicare, which only pays for skilled nursing, the Medicaid program will pay for long-term care in a nursing home once you've qualified. Medicare does not pay for treatment for all diseases or conditions. For example, Alzheimer's or Parkinson's disease may require a long-term stay in a nursing home and even though the patient receives medical care, Medicare will not pay for the treatment. These stays are called custodial nursing stays. Medicare does not pay for custodial nursing home stays. In that instance, you will either have to pay privately (i.e. use long-term care insurance or your own funds), or you will have to qualify for Medicaid.

Why Seek Advice for Medicaid?

As life expectancies and long-term care costs continue to rise, the challenge quickly becomes how to pay for these services. Many people cannot afford to pay $7,000 to $8,000 per month or more for the cost of a nursing home, and those who can pay for a while, may find their life savings wiped out in a matter of months. Fortunately, the Medicaid Program is there to help. In fact, in our lifetime, Medicaid has become the long-term care insurance of the middle class. But the eligibility to receive Medicaid benefits requires that you pass certain tests on the amount of income and assets that you have.

The reason to plan for Medicaid is two fold. First, you need to provide enough assets for the security of you, your spouse and loved ones — they too may have a similar crisis. Second, the rules are extremely complicated and confusing. The result is that without planning and advice, many people spend more than they should and their family security may be jeopardized.

Exempt Assets and Countable Assets: What Must Be Spent?

To qualify for Medicaid, applicants must pass some fairly strict tests on the amount of assets they can keep. To understand how Medicaid works, we first need to review what are known as exempt and non-exempt (or countable) assets. Exempt assets are those, which Medicaid will not take into account at least for the time being. In general, the following are the primary exempt assets:

• Home, equity up to $500,000. The home must be the principal place of residence. The nursing home resident may be required to show some "intent to return home," even if this never actually takes place

   • Personal belongings and household goods

   • One car or truck

   • Income-producing real estate

   • Burial spaces and certain related items for applicant and spouse

• Irrevocable prepaid funeral contract.

• Value of life insurance if face value is $1,500 or less. If it does exceed $1,500 in total face amount, then the cash value in these policies is countable.

All other assets are generally non-exempt, and are countable. Basically, all money and property and any item that can be valued and turned into cash, is a countable asset unless it is one of those assets listed above as exempt. This includes:

• Cash, savings, and checking accounts, credit union share and draft accounts

• Certificates of deposit

• U.S. Savings Bonds

• Individual Retirement Accounts (IRA), Keogh plans (401K, 403B) of the institutionalized spouse

• Prepaid funeral contracts which can be canceled

• Trusts (depending on the terms of the Trust)

• Real estate (other than the residence)

• More than one car

• Boats or recreational vehicles

• Stocks, bonds, or mutual funds

• Land contracts or mortgages held on real estate sold.

While the Medicaid rules themselves are complicated and tricky, it's safe to say a single person will qualify for Medicaid as long as he/she has only exempt assets plus a small amount of cash and/or money in the bank.

Some Common Questions

I've added my kids' names to our bank account. Do they still count? Yes. The entire amount is counted unless you can prove the other person who is on the account contributed some or all of the money. This rule applies to cash assets such as:

- Savings and checking accounts
- Credit union share and draft accounts
- Certificates of deposit
- U.S. Savings Bonds

Can't I Just Give My Assets Away?

Not under the new law. The answer is, maybe, but only if it's done just right. The law has severe penalties for people who simply give away their assets to create Medicaid eligibility. For example, every $6,757.67 given away during the three years prior to a Medicaid application creates a period of ineligibility of five (5) years. So even though the federal gift tax laws allow you to give away up to $13,000 per year without gift tax consequences, those gifts could result in a period of ineligibility.

In addition, legislation enacted on February 8, 2006, will extend the "look back" period to five years (and in some ways the penalty period) and impose other harsh new penalties for gifts made after February 8, 2006. Gifting under the new rules may be possible. However, it is critically important that you have the advice of an attorney well versed in these new rules. Any gift over $1,500 counts. This means that even if you pay a caregiver relative $1,000 per month with no personal service contract in place, this constitutes a gift that will penalize you for five years.

Division of Assets:
Medicaid Planning for Married Couples

Division of Assets is the name commonly used for the Spousal Impoverishment provisions of the Medicare Catastrophic Act of 1988. It applies only to couples. The intent of the law was to change the eligibility requirements for Medicaid where one spouse needs nursing home care while the other spouse remains in the community, i.e., at home. The law, in effect, recognizes that it makes little sense to impoverish both spouses when only one needs to qualify for Medicaid assistance for nursing home care. As a result of this recognition, division of assets was born.

Basically, in a division of assets, the couple gathers all of their countable assets together in a review. Exempt assets, discussed above, are not counted. The countable assets are then divided in two, with the at-home or "community spouse" allowed to keep one half of all countable assets to a maximum of approximately $104,400.00. The other half of the countable assets must be "spent down" until less than $2,400 or $8,000 remains depending on income. The amount of the countable assets that the at-home spouse gets to keep is called the Community Spouse Resource Allowance (CSRA).

Each state also establishes a monthly income for the at-home spouse. This is called the Minimum Monthly Maintenance Needs Allowance, which permits the community spouse to keep a minimum monthly income ranging from about $1,650 to $2,541. If the community spouse does not have at least $1,650 in income, then he or she is allowed to take the income of the nursing home spouse in an amount large enough to reach the Minimum Monthly Maintenance Needs Allowance (i.e., up to at least $1,650). The nursing home spouse's remaining income goes to the nursing home. This avoids the necessity (hopefully) for the at-home spouse to dip into savings each month, which would result in gradual impoverishment. To illustrate, assume the at-home spouse receives $800 per month in Social Security. Also assume that her needs are calculated to be the minimum of $1,650. With her Social Security, she is $850 short each month.

$1,650 at-home spouse's monthly needs (as determined by formula)

$800 at-home spouse's Social Security

$850 shortfall

In this case, the community spouse will receive $850 (the shortfall amount) per month from the nursing home spouse's Social Security and the rest of the nursing home spouse's income will then go to pay for the cost of his care. This does not mean, however, that there are no planning alternatives that the couple can pursue. Consider the following case studies:

Case Study: Medicaid Planning for Married People

Ralph and Alice were high school sweethearts who lived in Pittsburgh, PA their entire adult lives. Two weeks ago, Ralph and Alice celebrated their 51st anniversary. Yesterday, Alice, who has Alzheimer's, wandered away from home. Hours later she was found sitting on a street curb, talking incoherently. She was taken to a hospital and treated for dehydration. The family doctor tells Ralph he needs to place Alice in a nursing home. Ralph and Alice grew up during the Depression and have always tried to save something every month. Their assets, totaling $100,000, not including their house, are as follows:

Savings account	$15,000
CDs	$45,000
Money Market account	$37,000
Checking account	$3,000
Residence (no mortgage)	$80,000

Ralph gets Social Security and pension checks totaling $1,500 each month; Alice's check is $450. His eyes fill with tears as he says, "At $7,500 to the nursing home every month, our entire life savings will be gone in less than two years!" What's more, he's concerned he won't be able to pay her monthly nursing home bill because a neighbor told him that the nursing home would be entitled to all of their Social Security checks. However, there is good news for Ralph and Alice. It is possible he will get to keep his income and most of their assets and still have the state Medicaid program pay Alice's nursing home costs. While the process may take a little while, the end result will be worth it. To apply for Medicaid, he will have to go through the Pennsylvania Department of Public Welfare (DPW). If he does things strictly according to the way DPW tells him, he will only be able to keep about 1/2 of their assets (or about $50,000) and he will keep his income and house. But the results can actually be much better than the traditional spend-down, which everyone talks about.

Ralph might be able to turn the spend-down amount of roughly $50,000 into an income stream for him that will increase his income and meet the Medicaid spend- down almost immediately. In other words, if handled properly Alice may be eligible for Medicaid from the first month that she enters into the nursing home. Please note this will not work in every case. That's why it is important to have an Elder Law attorney guide you through the system and the Medicaid process to find the strategies that will be most beneficial in your situation.

Ralph will have to get advice from someone who knows how to navigate the system, but with proper advice he may be able to keep most of what he and Alice have worked so hard for. This is possible because the law does not intend to impoverish one spouse because the other needs care in a nursing home. This is certainly an example where knowledge of the rules and how to apply them can be used to resolve

Ralph and Alice's dilemma. Of course, proper Medicaid planning differs according to the relevant facts and circumstances of each situation as well as the state law.

Case Study: A Trust for a Disabled Child

Margaret and Sam have always taken care of their daughter, Elizabeth. She is 45, has never worked, and has never left home. She is "developmentally disabled" and receives Supplemental Security Income (SSI). They have always worried about who will care for her after they die. Some years ago, Sam was diagnosed with Dementia. His health has deteriorated to the point that Margaret can no longer take care of him. Now she has placed Sam in a nursing home and is paying $7,800 per month out of savings. Margaret is even more worried that there will not be any money left for the care of Elizabeth. Margaret is satisfied with the nursing home Sam is in. The facility has a Medicaid bed available that Sam could have if he were eligible. Medicaid would pay his bill. However, according to the information she got from the social worker, Sam is $48,000 away from Medicaid eligibility. Margaret wishes there was a way to save the $48,000 for Elizabeth after she and Sam are gone.

There is a way to save the $48,000 for Elizabeth's needs. Margaret can consult an Elder Law attorney to set up a "Special Needs Trust" with the $48,000 to provide for Elizabeth. As soon as Margaret transfers the money to the Trust, Sam will be eligible for Medicaid. Elizabeth will not lose her benefits, and her Supplemental Security Income is assured. Of course, all Trusts must be reviewed for compliance with Medicaid rules. Also, failure to report assets is fraud, and when discovered, will cause loss of eligibility and repayment of benefits and perhaps even impose criminal penalties.

I Heard I Can Give Away $13,000 Per Year. Can I?

As discussed earlier, many people have heard of the federal gift tax provision that allows them to give away $13,000 per year without paying any gift taxes. What they do not know is that this refers to a gift tax exemption. It is not an absolute right where Medicaid is concerned. Having heard of the exemption, they wonder, "Can't I give my assets away?" Perhaps, but only if it's done within the strict allowances of the law. So even though the federal Gift Tax law allows you to give away up to $13,000 per year without incurring tax, those gifts over $500 could result in a Medicaid period of ineligibility for five years. Still, some parents want to make gifts to their children before their life savings are all gone. Next, consider the following case study:

Case Study: Financial Gifts to Children

After her 73-year-old husband, Harold, suffers a paralyzing stroke, Mildred and her daughter, Joan, need advice. Dark circles have formed under Mildred's eyes. Her hair is disheveled. Joan holds her hand. "The doctor says

Harold needs long-term care in a nursing home," Mildred says. "I have some money in savings, but not enough. I don't want to lose my house and all our hard-earned money. I don't know what to do.

Joan has heard about Medicaid benefits for nursing homes, but doesn't want her mother left destitute in order for Harold to qualify for them. Joan wants to ensure that her father's medical needs are met, but she also wants to preserve Mildred's assets. "Can't Mom just give her money to me as a gift?" she asks. "Can't she give away $13,000 a year? I could keep the money for her so she doesn't lose it when Dad applies for Medicaid.

Joan has confused general estate and tax laws with the issue of asset transfers and Medicaid eligibility. A "gift" to a child in this case is actually a transfer, and Medicaid has very specific rules about transfers. At the time Harold applies for Medicaid, for gifts made prior to February 8, 2006, the state will "look-back" three years to see if any gifts have been made. Gifts made after February 8, 2006 will be subject to a five-year look-back. The state won't let you just give away your money or your property to qualify for Medicaid. Any gifts or transfers for less than fair market value that are uncovered in the look-back period will cause a delay in Harold's eligibility for Medicaid. In addition to the changes in the look-back period from three to five years, the new law also states that the penalty period on asset transfers will not begin until the Medicaid applicant is in the nursing home and already spent down. This will frustrate the gifting plans of most people.

So what can Harold and Mildred do? They may be able to institute a gifting program, save a good portion of their estate, and still qualify for Medicaid. But they have to set it up just right. The new rules are very technical and unclear. You should consult a knowledgeable advisor on how this may be done.

Will I Lose My Home?

People who apply for medical assistance benefits to pay for nursing home care ask this question. For many, their home constitutes much or most of their life savings. Often, it's the only asset that a person has to pass on to his or her children. Under the Medicaid regulations, the home is an exempt asset so long as equity is less than $500,000. This means that it is not taken into account when calculating eligibility for Medicaid. But in 1993, Congress passed a little-debated law that affects hundreds of thousands of families with a spouse or elderly parent in a nursing home. That law requires states to try to recover the value of Medicaid payments made to nursing home residents. Estate recovery does not take place until the recipient of the benefits dies (or until both spouses are deceased if it is a married couple). Then, federal law requires that the states attempt to recover the benefits paid from the recipient's probate and in some cases non-probate estate. Generally, the probate estate consists of assets that the deceased owned in his or her name alone without beneficiary designation. The non-probate assets include assets owned jointly or payable to a beneficiary.

About two-thirds of the nation's nursing home residents have their costs paid in part by Medicaid. Obviously, the Estate Recovery law affects many families. The asset most frequently caught in the Estate Recovery web is the home of the Medicaid recipient. A nursing home resident can often own a home and receive Medicaid benefits without having to sell the home. But upon death, if the home is part of the probate or non-probate estate, the state may seek to force the sale of the home in order to reimburse the state for the payments that were made.

Legal Assistance

Aging persons and their family members face many unique legal issues. As you can tell from our discussion of the Medicaid program, the legal, financial, and care planning issues facing the prospective nursing home resident and family can be particularly complex. If you or a family member needs nursing home care, it is clear that you need legal help. Where can you turn for that help?

It is difficult for the consumer to be able to identify lawyers who have the training and experience required to provide guidance during this most difficult time. Generally, nursing home planning and Medicaid planning is an aspect of the services provided by Elder Law attorneys. Consumers must be cautious in choosing a lawyer and carefully investigate the lawyer's credentials. How do you find a law office that has the knowledge and experience you need? You may want to start with recommendations from friends who have received professional help with nursing home issues. Which law firm did they use? Were they satisfied with the services they received? Hospital social workers, Alzheimer and other support groups, accountants, and other financial professionals can also be good sources of recommendations. In general, a lawyer who devotes a substantial part of his or her practice to nursing home planning should have more knowledge and experience to address the issues properly. Don't hesitate to ask the lawyer what percentage of his or her practice involves nursing home planning. Or you may want to ask how many new nursing home planning cases the law office handles each month. There is no correct answer. But there is a good chance that a law office that assists with two nursing home placements a week is likely to be more up-to-date and knowledgeable than an office that helps with two placements a year.

Ask whether the lawyer is a member of any Elder Law planning organizations. Is the lawyer involved with committees or local or state bar organizations that have to do with nursing home planning? If so, has the lawyer held a position of authority on the committee? Does the lawyer lecture on nursing home planning? If so, to whom? For example, if the lawyer is asked to teach other lawyers about Elder Law and nursing home planning, that is a very good sign that the lawyer is considered to be knowledgeable. If the lawyer offers lectures to the public, you might try to attend one of the seminars. This should help you decide if this lawyer can serve your needs. The leading national organization of Elder Law attorneys is the National Academy of Elder Law Attorneys (NAELA), 1604 North Country Club Road, Tucson, Arizona. While mere membership in the Academy is open to any lawyer and is no sure sign that the attorney is an experienced Elder Law practitioner, membership does at least show that the lawyer has some interest in the field. In addition, the Academy runs three-day educational sessions twice each year to help lawyers stay current on the latest aspects of elder law and nursing home planning. Attending these sessions takes time and commitment on the part of the lawyer and is a good sign that the lawyer is attempting to stay up to date on nursing home issues. You may want to look for an attorney who is a member of NAELA and has recently attended one or more of its educational sessions. In the end, follow your instincts and choose an attorney who knows this area of the law, who is committed to helping others, and who will listen to you and the unique wants and needs of you and your family.

CHAPTER 10
SECRET VETERANS BENEFITS

As Elder Law attorneys, many of us have only recently learned how to help clients who may need an important Veterans Administration benefit available to wartime veterans who may be facing substantial medical care expense. A veteran who is confined to his or her home or needs assisted living facility care may qualify for benefits. Secretary Nicholson of the Department of Veterans Affairs recently reported that the VA is reaching out to veterans and spouses to alert them to an under-used benefit called "Aid and Attendance" (A and A). It has been reported by the VA that thousands of veterans may not be receiving the VA disability benefits to which they are entitled. One of the VA's best-kept secrets, which is an excellent potential source of funds for long-term care either at home or in an assisted living facility are veteran's benefits for a non-service connected disability. Most VA benefits and pensions are based on a disability that was incurred during a veteran's wartime service.

This particular benefit is available for individuals who are disabled due to the issues of old age, such as Alzheimer's, Parkinson's, Multiple Sclerosis, and other physical disabilities, not a service related disability. For those veterans and the surviving spouse of a veteran who are eligible, these benefits can be a blessing for the disabled individual who is not yet ready for a nursing home. This benefit can be as high as $1,949.00 per month for a married veteran, for a single veteran, $1644.00 and for widows and widowers of a veteran, $1,099.00. This money can potentially be used for home Healthcare or assisted living facilities. We were shocked to learn that thousands of veterans may be missing out on this valuable benefit, which they have a legal right to receive.

The pension benefits provided by the Veterans Administration generally fall into two categories: service connected and non-service connected. We will focus on non-service connected benefits which are available to certain wartime veterans (or their dependents) who are disabled because of a non-service connected condition and who are in financial need due to their unreimbursed medical expenses. Once the veteran's eligibility requirements are met, a family member may be able to obtain benefits based on his or her status as the veteran's dependent.

Most VA benefits and pensions are based upon a disability that was incurred during a veteran's wartime service. This particular benefit is available for individuals who are disabled due to issues of old age, such as Alzheimer's, Parkinson's, Multiple Sclerosis, but not for service-related disabilities. For those veterans and widows/widowers who are eligible, this benefit can be a blessing for the disabled individual who is not yet ready for a nursing home. The money can be used for home Healthcare or an assisted living facility. It is not generally used for nursing home costs.

There is a specific portion of the pension program, which is of particular importance. This program is "Aid and Attendance" (A and A) and is available to a veteran who is not only disabled, but also has the additional requirement of needing the aid and attendance of another person in order to avoid the hazards of his or her daily environment. What that means in English is someone needs to help you to prepare meals, to bathe, to dress and otherwise take care of yourself. Under this program, a married veteran can receive a maximum of $1,949.00 per month in benefits and a widow or widower can receive up to $1,099.00, and a single veteran can receive up to $1,644.00 as a maximum benefit for A and A for the year 2009. The applicant must be judged to be "permanently and totally disabled". The applicant does not need to be helpless – he/she need only show that he/she is in need of aid and attendance on a regular basis. Someone who is housebound or in an assisted living facility and over the age of 65 is presumed by the Veterans Administration to be in need of aid and attendance.

CHAPTER 11
CONCLUSION

We hope we have opened your eyes to some issues. The best consumer is an informed consumer. You are now not an attorney, but you are an informed consumer who knows more about estate planning than most attorneys.

Before completing an estate plan, we strongly recommend that you contact an accountant and an elder law estate planning attorney.

Remember, you only have one shot at doing this right, so do it right the first time. The biggest enemy of estate planning is Procrastination! So do something. Doing something is always better than nothing.

Now that you have educated yourself, the rest is up to you. It's up to you to find the right lawyer for your estate plan.

Take Action.

Be Persistent.

Ask Questions.

The Best of Luck to You and God Bless.

APPENDIX A
ESTATE ORGANIZER

SCHEDULES OF ASSETS
AND
OTHER INFORMATION

GENERAL INFORMATION TO OUR FAMILY

1) MISCELLANEOUS:

a) Our safe deposit box is located at:

_____

b) The keys to the safe deposit box are located at:

_____

c) Someone else's property is in our safe deposit box.

_____'s property is identifiable as:

_____

d) We have someone else's property in our possession.

_____'s property is identifiable as:

_____

e) Our personal safe is located at:

_____

f) Our tax records are located at:

_____

g) Other:

_____

2) ADVISORS:

[We suggest that you complete this section in pencil so that changes can be made as necessary.]

NAME	ADDRESS	TELEPHONE
*Personal Representative(s)		
*Trustee(s)		
Attorney		
Doctor		
Religious Advisor		

Guardian		
CPA		
Insurance Agent		
Stockbroker		

*Other than Husband or Wife

GENERAL INFORMATION TO MY FAMILY FROM_____

1) DIRECTIONS FOR MEMORIAL SERVICES:

_____

_____

_____

_____

_____

_____

2) BURIAL:

My body should be buried in_____

cemetery located in_____

My body should be cremated and the ashes

_____

My body should be donated to

_____

Other, specify

_____

3) SPECIFIC COMMENTS, WISHES, THOUGHTS:

_____

_____

_____

GENERAL INFORMATION TO MY FAMILY FROM_____

1) DIRECTIONS FOR MEMORIAL SERVICES:

_____

_____

_____

_____

_____

_____

2) BURIAL:

My body should be buried in_____

cemetery located in_____

My body should be cremated and the ashes

_____

My body should be donated to

_____

Other, specify

_____

3) SPECIFIC COMMENTS, WISHES, THOUGHTS:

_____

_____

_____

SPECIFIC LIST OF ASSETS

[It would be very helpful to your family if this list is kept up-to-date.]

Keep a copy of Certificates of Deposit with this page.

Location of originals:_____

BANK ACCOUNTS

INCLUDE CHECKING, SAVINGS, CERTIFICATES OF DEPOSIT, ETC.

NAME AND ADDRESS OF INSTITUTION	TYPE OF ACCOUNT	ACCOUNT NUMBER

SPECIFIC LIST OF ASSETS

[It would be very helpful to your family if this list is kept up-to-date.]

Keep a copy of stock certificates with this page.

Location of originals:_____

STOCK

NAME OF CORPORATION	NAME & ADDRESS OF BROKER/TRANSFER AGENT	ACCOUNT NUMBER OR CERTIFICATE#

SPECIFIC LIST OF ASSETS

[It would be very helpful to your family if this list is kept up-to-date.]

Keep a copy of bonds with this page.

Location of originals:

BONDS

TYPE OF BOND	NAME & ADDRESS OF AGENT TO CONTACT	BOND OR ACCOUNT NUMBER

SPECIFIC LIST OF ASSETS

[It would be very helpful to your family if this list is kept up-to-date.]

Keep a copy of all notes, land contracts in which you are a creditor, etc. with this page.

Location of originals:_____

ACCOUNTS RECEIVABLE

NAME AND ADDRESS OF DEBTOR	DUE DATE OF PAYMENT	SECURITY FOR DEBT

SPECIFIC LIST OF ASSETS

[It would be very helpful to your family if this list is kept up-to-date.]

Keep copies of evidence of any business assets and business agreements with this page (e.g., partnership agreements, buy-sell agreements, close corporation stock certificates, and miscellaneous business agreements).

Location of originals:_____

BUSINESS ASSETS

TYPE OF ASSET	LOCATION OF ASSET	ACCOUNT NUMBER OR ID NUMBER

SPECIFIC LIST OF ASSETS

[It would be very helpful to your family if this list is kept up-to-date.]

Keep copies of all deeds with this page.

Location of originals:_____

REAL ESTATE

ADDRESS	TYPE OF PROPERTY

SPECIFIC LIST OF ASSETS

[It would be very helpful to your family if this list is kept up-to-date.]

Keep copies of all titles with this page.

Location of originals:_____

TITLED PROPERTY

INCLUDE CARS, TRUCKS, CAMPERS, BOATS, MOTORCYCLES, MOBILE HOMES, ETC.

YEAR	MAKE	MODEL	STATE WHERE TITLED

SPECIFIC LIST OF ASSETS

[Please list any information which may be of importance regarding any other assets.]

Location of originals:_____

OTHER ASSETS

_____

_____

_____

_____

_____

_____

_____

_____

_____

_____

_____

_____

_____

_____

_____

_____

SCHEDULE OF LIFE INSURANCE/TAX-DEFERRED ANNUITIES

Include copies of the face page of insurance policies.

Location of originals:_____

COMPANY	PERSON INSURED	BENEFICIARY DESIGNATIONS PRIMARY	CONTINGENT
LIFE INSURANCE (Include accidental death policies)			
ANNUITIES			

SCHEDULE OF OTHER TYPES OF INSURANCE

Include copies of the face page of insurance policies.

Location of originals:_____

TYPE	COMPANY	AMOUNT AND TYPE OF BENEFITS
DISABILITY		
MEDICAL		
AUTO		
HOMEOWNERS		
OTHER LIABILITY		
OTHER		

SCHEDULE OF TAX-DEFERRED INVESTMENTS

Include copies of the face page of policies, agreements, etc.

Location of originals:_____

| | COMPANY | BENEFICIARY DESIGNATIONS | |
		PRIMARY	CONTINGENT
PENSION			
PROFIT SHARING			
I.R.A.'s			
KEOGHS			
TAX-DEFERRED ANNUITIES			
OTHER			

The Elder Law Offices of Shields & Boris serves all of Western Pennsylvania in the areas of Estate planning and Elder Law. Together Attorney's James P. Shields and Thomas J. Boris have over 19 years of legal experience and have helped over a thousand families, couples and individuals with estate planning, Wills, Trusts, Powers of Attorney, Living Wills, probate, special needs planning, Medicaid planning and asset protection from nursing homes.

Attorney Shields and Attorney Boris are members of the National Academy of Elder Law Attorneys, the Pennsylvania Bar Association, Allegheny County Bar Association, NESA, and many other national professional organizations.

About James P. Shields: Attorney Shields graduated cum laude from Saint Francis College in 1990 and from the University of Notre Dame Law School in 1993. He is admitted to the Pennsylvania Bar and Ohio Bar. Jim and his wife Denise have resided in Western Pennsylvania their entire lives and have five children.

About Thomas J. Boris: Attorney Boris is a graduate of Washington & Jefferson College (1994) and Duquesne University School of Law (2001). He is admitted to the Pennsylvania Bar and the U.S. District court for the Western District of Pennsylvania. Tom and his wife Stephanie have resided in Western Pennsylvania their entire lives and have two children.